FOREX TRADING

IN THE ASIAN MARKET

¥€$

Table of Contents

Introduction

Today all the top Forex traders are aware that consistent profits can be only made by identifying the markets that are emerging. Since Forex deals with the lowest common denominator for any country, it is important to get knowledge about how these diverse trading systems operate. Apart from understanding the dynamics in international relationships it is also important to understand the dynamics of their market trades. Today India and China have emerged as the fastest growing economies of the world.

It can be said that as liquidity gets restored to the Forex market, with the weekend passing, all Asian markets are of course the first to see action. Basically, unofficial activity from the Asian continent is still dominated, and represented by the markets of Tokyo. This capital market is live from midnight till almost 6am Greenwich Mean Time. But there are also many other countries that have their share of considerable pull. Their hold over this period is getting stronger, and these include India and China. The non-Asian markets that manage to get this hold include New Zealand, Australia and Russia, among others.

Since these markets are all scattered, this is also the reason for starting and ending the stretched Asian session beyond the standard Tokyo work hours. This permits different markets activities levels, even though Asian hours generally get restricted between 11pm and 8am GMT.

The role of the U.S and China has also been termed as "Chimerica", by Niall Ferguson, who wrote "Te Ascent of Money." The term describes the delicate relation that exists between these two great economies. As per the CIA World Fact book, U.S remains the largest economy in the world. Japan ranks second and China ranks third. However, it is expected that Japan would lose its position in the second place, and get taken over by China. As the demands for Chinese goods keeps growing in the U.S by almost more than 500%, as compared to the demand for U.S products, the Asian Forex markets are enjoying the boom of this economy.

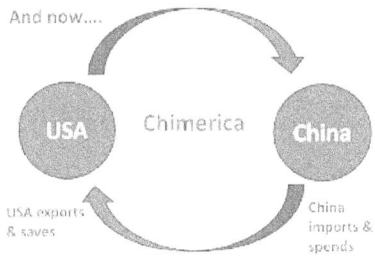

Asian options and its history

An Asian option is a term used in finance, and is also referred to as average option. Basically this is an option where the payoff is linked to an average value of the underlier. This happens on a specific set of dates, in the tenure or life of the option. Asian options have two basic categories which include the average rate option and the average strike option. The average rate option is also called the average price option, where a cash-settled option, with its payoff is based on differences between an average value of the underlier and its fixed strike, during the life of the option.

The average strike option has been known as cash settled or physically settled option. This option is a structured form like a vanilla option but here its strike is set at the same level like the average value of the underlier, during the entire life of the option. Both of these forms can be altered or structured according to puts and calls. Even though exercise is mainly European, there are ways for specifying early exercise provisions, which are dependent on an average-to-date. Both of these averages can be calculated arithmetically and geometrically.

Actually the term Asian option is of no meticulous significance. According to facts, David Spaughton and Mark Standish, who worked in Tokyo in the Bankers Trust in 1987, developed the primary commercially used price formula for options, and then linked it to the average price of crude oil. Since they had completed this process in Asia, the name Asian options were used here.

The end-users of energies or commodities have a tendency to be exposed to standard prices over time. Hence these Asian options are attractive to such commodities and they are also popular with corporations. Mainly exporters with ongoing currency exposures prefer using these Asian options. These Asian options are also attractive as they are less expensive and usually sell at lower premiums, when compared with vanilla puts or calls.

Costs of these Asian options are lower because volatility, with the average value of an underlier, is usually on the lower side. There are many situations where an underlier could be thinly traded or have potential manipulation of process, and thus Asian option offers them with a certain level of protection. Usually the manipulation of the average value this option can get difficult for the underlier, over an extended period of time. However, it is easier to manipulate these options at the time of the expiration of an option.

An Asian option can also be defined as a special type of option contract. For Asian options, payoffs may be determined or evaluated through average underlying prices, which are pre-set over a certain period of time. This process is much different, as compared to the case of regular European and American options. In the latter, payoff of the option contract is largely dependent on costs of the underlying instrument during period of maturity. A benefit of the Asian options is that they help in reducing risk of market manipulation at maturity.

This is one of the most common questions that are being asked to financial experts around the world. Before entering into more details about the working of principles of Forex, and their technicalities, let us understand a basic overview of this question. Basically the significance of this question would be to enjoy becoming an astute investor. Experts agree that there is a need to follow places where the hot money is. And currently it includes the Indian and Chinese markets.

Experts from around the world are agreeing that the hot money is indeed going to be in the Asian market for the next few years, and is expected to retain its position there. The trading Asian currencies are not the only solution for investing in these markets. For instance, the spread for both the SGD and JPY, which are both Asian currencies, is 15 pips!

Hence, why would you be interested in trading that alone and wait for the market to move 16 pips, and in your direction it would be much before you could even register a profit.

The answer here would be observing the currencies which will help you understand if Asia is doing well. Hence, the focus here should be on the commodity currencies of AUD, NZD and CAD. They are only some of the currencies that would strengthen significantly grow stronger over their counterparts in the coming few years.

Understanding payouts for Asian call options through Mathematical average

Payouts for the Asian options can be defined in many different ways and here continuous case provide a payout equation of-

$\text{max}\left(\frac{1}{T} \int_{0}^{T} S(t)\, dt - K, 0\right)$.

Here T is the time up to expiry; S would be price while K is the strike price.

In cases of discrete monitoring the payout would be $\text{max}\left(\frac{1}{N} \sum_{i=1}^{N} S(t_i) - K, 0\right)$

If the monitoring at the times is $t_1, t_2, \dots, t_n$

Asian options can be derived using both geometric averages along with arithmetic average. The Asian options help to understand and discuss problem of pricing Asian options, in concern with Monte Carlo. There are different approaches used here for solving these issues by renowned analysts and financial experts.

Here, the Variance Gamma model may be implemented efficiently in pricing Asian style options. The use of Bondesson series representation is suggested in generating the variance gamma processes, which have revealed some advantages in pricing these Asian options. Here, determining the exercise price would be the key to understanding the working of Asian options. For arriving at the exercise price, identification of the average price, for the concerned underlying security, over a specified period is required. For instance, the price activity for an underlying security, over six months to 12 months, may be charted. Here the average price would be calculated from that data, and as this average is determined, static discounts may be applied to that figure.

The other option that may be used in Asian options is the Asian quanto-basket option. This is actually a contract that permits an investor to participate in return of an industrial or economic sector, via an international exposure, but without foreign exchange risk exposition. It has been seen that payoffs of these contracts would also include sums of lognormal random variables. However, there is no analytical solution available for computing its price and thus many financial experts have examined precision of three different analytical approximations to compute the same. These models can be computed in fractions of seconds to get the Asian quanto-basket option.

Here the analysis would reveal the fact that the Johnson approximation has been suggested as the most precise method and the preferred method for lognormal and gamma inverse approximations. However, it should be pointed out that these convergences have association with non-linear algorithm, and this is required to be monitored closely for getting successful approximations. Even though failures to this converge do not happen frequently, there is a possibility that it could lead to substantial errors, if they had been undetected. Another option for getting these approximations would be the gamma inverse approximation, which has been known for revealing excellent results and has the precision required for most practical situations.

There are various reasons for the popularity of the Asian options and one of them includes risk-free benefits. Generally these Asian options are considered to be investment opportunities, which carry a very moderate amount of risk. This happens since the processing or determining of exercise price includes collection of data about performance of the security, over a particular duration of time. Hence it can be stated that it is relatively easy to decide if Asian options would be apt for fulfilling the investment goals of an investor.

Usually conservative investors are more comfortable with options if there security appears to be more volatile, and the process of calculation in Asian options makes these factors visibly clear. This permits the investors to seek opportunities elsewhere and those who specialize in high risk ventures are able to understand that an Asian option would probably not be able to give a potential for the level of return. This these investors seeking such deals could move to riskier investments, which would also have a potentially higher rate of return.

These Asian options would be a viable investment option for various sorts of individual and corporate investors. These options provide what may be termed as an equitable amount of risk, which is matched with a rational return. Asian options continue to be lucrative for many people, who seek creativity with their investments, even as they are able to avoid high speculative deals.

Different ways for pricing Asian options

There are different methods of pricing Asian options, and they are regularly updated, and evaluated, with new additions and equations are being added to the same. These include-

1. Geometric Closed Form or the Kemna & Vorst 1990

Kemna and Vorst brought forward a closed form pricing solution for getting geometric averaging options. This was done by altering volatility and the cost of carry term. Basically these geometric averaging options may be priced through some closed form analytic solution. This happens because of the geometric average of the underlying prices following lognormal distribution. However, the arithmetic average rate options result in this condition collapsing.

Geometric averaging Asian call and puts are given as:

$$c_G = Se^{(\delta-r)(T-t)} N(d_1) - Xe^{-r(T-t)} N(d_2)$$

And $p_G = Xe^{-r(T-t)} N(-d_2) - Se^{(\delta-r)(T-t)} N(-d_1)$

Here N(x) would be cumulative normal distribution function, which may be simplified further.

$$d_1 = \frac{\ln |{}^S\!/\!_X| + |b + 0.5\sigma_A^2| T}{\sigma_A \sqrt{T}}$$

$$d_2 = \frac{\ln |{}^S\!/\!_X| + |b - 0.5\sigma_A^2| T}{\sigma_A \sqrt{T}}$$

Adjusted volatility and dividend yield would be

$$\sigma_A = \frac{\sigma}{\sqrt{3}}$$

$$b = \frac{1}{2}\left(r - D - \frac{\sigma^2}{6}\right)$$

Here σ would be the observed volatility, r is equal to risk free rate of interest and D would be dividend yield.

2. Arithmetic Rate Approximation, devised by Turnbull & Wakeman in1991

Since there are no closed form solutions available for arithmetic averages there are plenty of approximations, which have emerged in literature. This happened because of the inappropriate use of some lognormal assumption, in reference with this form of averaging. Suggested by Turnbull and Wakeman, or TW, in 1991, this approximation makes use of the knowledge that distribution beneath arithmetic averaging would be approximately lognormal. Hence they made an attempt to put forward the first and second moments for averages, for getting to price the option.

3) Arithmetic Rate Approximation

This arithmetic rate approximation was put forward by Levy, which is another analytical approximation suggesting giving more accurate results, as compared with the TW approximation.

4) Arithmetic Rate Approximation

Curran had produced an approximation of the arithmetic rate based on Asian options in 1992. This had been done on a geometric conditioning approach where the model is aimed towards knowledge of the geometric distribution, along with underlying asset price, at any given time. Considering the natural logarithm for both these aspects, at any given point of time, can be used for conditioning underlying asset prices. The geometric distribution and integration are done accordingly.

5) Binomial Method and Trinomial Trees

Similar to many other options, these Asian options may also be priced through lattice or tree methods. However, an additional consideration which should be adhered to, at any given point of time, would be the fact that the value of an option is reliant upon on an average of the price, and which path should be taken. Considering the averaging nature of Asian options the minimum and maximum range at each node can be determined. This would be dependent on the path for which an underlying asset had been taken.

The problem here would be that with the growing number of nodes on a tree, the numbers of averages also grow. Hence this should be taken into account, especially with the central nodes. This is vital because any number of averages, which are taken here, would be exponentially related to a certain number of possible asset paths. Hull and White had made an attempt to solve this problem even in 1993, with addition of a state variable to the tree nodes. In such cases the approximation would be undertaken with interpolation techniques, which move with backward induction.

6) Finite Differences Technique

There are so many different papers, which document the use of finite differences and use them for solving Asian options. These had been published since the early-mid 90s where Rogers & Shi had presented a technique, which used a one dimensional PDE. This can be used for solving finite differences but this method is also prone to problems. Basically these are problems associated with the diffusion term, lower volatilities and short durations of maturities. Andreasen had expanded on Rogers & Shi's model in 1998 through the change of numeraire, for solving price of Asian options numerically. There are many kinds of infinite differences methods and applications for Asian options, which have been seen in Tavella & Randall, for the year 2000.

7) Arithmetic Rate Approximation or the Monte Carlo Simulation

There are plenty of ways to use Monte Carlo simulation method, which is also referred to as MCS. This had been developed for pricing arithmetic Asian options. This is actually an aforementioned analytical approximation by experts like Levy, TW and Curran, which may be computed using a simulation method. This simulation offers relatively accurate prices for the option values, with tremendous success for Asian options, which are very much path dependent.

A geometric closed form solution had been originally presented by Kemna & Vorst along with a solution for pricing arithmetic rate. There is also the control variant technique used with accurate analytical solutions for derivative prices, with similar and known analytic solution.

8) Monte Carlo or the Quasi-Monte Carlo

Basically the MCS methods had been used in various Asian options pricing but the general idea had been that they were not particularly effective for pricing Asian options, considering its terms of computational speed. Through the utilization of control or antithetic variable techniques, there was a chance of improving the accuracy of MCS methods. This could be done using closed form geometric average rate formula for the control variates.

QMCS method has been devised through use of quasi-random number sequences, which further help with the accuracy. But it has been seen in numerous papers that convergence would not be predominantly stable, particularly with exotic Asian options and thus would not be considered as an effective pricing method.

9) Other Methods

In finance, one of the major problems in finding solutions for various arithmetic rate Asian options would be the fact that these models fail to address the error bound association of solving the pricing problem. These would include the methods suggested by Milevsky & Posner who solved problems using Gamma and Johnson distributions. Geman & Yor would apply the Laplace transform and numerical inversion, but would fail to address the error bounds.

What are the Monte Carlo method and its role in Asian options?

The Monte Carlo methods may be defined as a kind or type of computational algorithms, which are largely dependent on repeated unsystematic sampling, which can be computed for getting their results. These Monte Carlo methods have been used in various streams, apart from finance, like physics, chemistry, etc. This method has been used for both simulating corporeal and mathematical systems. The method is popular because of its reliance on frequent computation, along with the derivation of random or even pseudo-random numbers.

Basically the Monte Carlo methods are ideally suited to calculation via the computer. These methods are used when it is unworkable or impracticable to compute a precise result, using the deterministic algorithm. Monte Carlo simulation techniques are viable for various studying programs and systems, considering their huge number of coupled degrees of autonomy. These would be applicable for cellular structures, fluids, and strongly coupled solids along with disordered materials.

On a broader connotation the Monte Carlo method can be used for modeling phenomenon but with significant indecision in its inputs. These would be applicable to the risks of calculation in business and other similar issues. Basically the Monte Carlo method has been extensively used in mathematics for evaluating definite integrals like the multidimensional integrals with complex boundary conditions. This has been considered as a largely safe method for risk analysis, compared to alternative methods or even intuitions. Apart from derivatives and options, these Monte Carlo simulations were applied in space and oil exploration.

Monte Carlo method had been formulated in the 1940s by a renowned physicist of Los Alamos National Laboratory, who had been working on nuclear weapon projects. Actually there is no single or unique Monte Carlo method but the term has been used for describing a huge and widely-used division of approaches. Monte Carlo methods use a particular set of patterns, which can be described as-

- Defining a domain with possible inputs
- Generation of random inputs from these domains
- Performance of deterministic computation via use of inputs
- Aggregating results of distinct computations in to the concluding results

All financial and mathematical applications of the Monte Carlo methods are based on valuation and analyzing portfolios, instruments and investments through stimulation of various sources. There is uncertainty, which affects their value, and the determination of their average values, as per range of resultant outcomes, are done on these bases. Benefits of the Monte Carlo methods over other techniques grow with dimensions of the problem increase.

Monte Carlo methods had been introduced in finance by David B. Hertz in 1964, through his work "Risk Analysis in Capital Investment" in the Harvard Business Review. This paper had discussed application of the Monte Carlo method in Corporate Finance. Phelim Boyle had pioneered the use of simulation in derivative valuation in 1977, through his seminal paper called "Options: A Monte Carlo Approach" in the journal of Financial Economics.

Uses of Monte Carlo methods

There are plenty of uses of the Monte Carlo methods and these include portfolio, investments and instrument.

The method had been used by financial analysts for constructing various stochastic or probabilistic financial models. These models in finance were opposed to the traditional static and deterministic models. These had been used to analyze characteristics of the project's net present value or NPV; cash flow components affected by uncertainty were modeled, along with a mathematical reflection of random characteristics. The above average NPV for a potential investment, along with volatility and other sensitivities could be observed from the resultant histogram, which was affective in the project's probability distribution, and permitted the estimation of the net present value greater than zero.

The Monte Carlo method had been useful in valuing an option on equity. Here the simulation would help to generate thousands of possible but random price paths, in concern with their underlying share. The associated exercise value or payoff for each path would be averaged and discounted to present date. Hence the result would be value of the option today.

This method is largely used for valuing bonds, and other options with the underlying source of uncertainty, which may be stimulated in short rate. This helped to get the annualized interest rate, which could be borrowed by an entity for a given period of time. Hence every evolution of interest rates would yield diverse curve results, and a different resultant bond price. For determining bond value, these prices would be averaged, and help to get value of bond option and equity options. Similar kinds of approaches had been used in valuing swaps and swaptions.

The Monte Carlo Methods has been used for evaluation of portfolio where each simulation and correlated behavior of factors that influence the component instruments, could be stimulated over time. Along with these factors the values of the instruments could be calculated and its portfolio value could also be observed. These portfolio values would be joined in a histogram and its statistical characteristics would be observed.

Monte Carlo methods are used for various kinds of personal financial planning and provide flexibility, along with handling multiple sources of indecision. But the techniques are nevertheless it not always suitable and used over other methods only with more than a few state variables.

Different levels of complexities and advantages of Monte Carlo methods

There are many problems entailing mathematical finance and their computation for a meticulous integral. For example, the issues of finding arbitrage free worth of some derivative. There are many instances where integrals can be valued analytically, along with a growing number of instances where they are valued by means of numerical integration. They can also be computed through a partial differential equation, which is also referred to as PDE.

It should be kept in mind that there are numeral dimensions, or levels of freedom, which create a huge problem. The PDE and numerical integrals usually get intractable here and in such instances, Monte Carlo methods provide better results.

There are various aspects to the Monte Carlo methods and usually formulae like the Black Scholes analytical solutions, don't exist for more than three or four state variables. The other standard approaches or the numerical methods like the Binomial options pricing form, or even the Finite difference techniques, go through many difficulties and hence are impractical. Hence, in these instances, the Monte Carlo methods are able to find the solution much faster, as compared to these numerical methods. The Monte Carlo methods also required lesser remembrance and are less difficult to program. But in many of the easier situations, simulation may not be an apt solution since it can get very time-consuming and exhausting computationally.

Control variate methods and Monte Carlo methods

Often it is feasible and practical to use the control variate in the Monte Carlo methods. For example, if you want to get the Monte Carlo value of any derivative B, but are aware of a value, which is an analytically similar derivative A. Then B* = (depicting the value of B according to Monte Carlo) + C*[(The value of A analytically) – (Value of A as per the same Monte Carlo methods)] would be a better approximation and CB is covar(B,A)/var(B).

The basic idea behind the technique, when it is applied for derivatives would be to mark that foundation of the variance, for a particular derivative, would be unswervingly dependent on their risks, which could be delta and Vega, for that particular derivative. This happens due to the fact that any mistake on the estimator, and for the onward rate of an underlier, would be generating a corresponding blunder. This would also be dependent on the delta of that particular derivative, in reference with its forward value. One of the best instances for demonstrating the same would be comparing an error when you are pricing the call and the put, which would have a much subordinate delta.

Hence, it may be stated that a normal way of selecting the derivative A would be to choose a replicating portfolio of alternatives for B. In this reference, one can price B without variance lessening. Here, calculating deltas and Vegas, by using combinations of calls and puts would result in similar control variates for deltas and Vegas.

What is importance sampling?

Another vital tool of the Monte Carlo Method would be importance sampling, which basically consists stimulates this method, using a dissimilar probability distribution. This has also been known as a modification of measure, which would offer more probability for the simulated underlier, so that they can be identified in locations where the derivative would payoff and have maximum convexity. For instance, you can get very near too the strike with instances of any simple option.

In these cases, replicated payoffs are not just averaged, like the basic methods of Monte Carlo. However, these are initially multiplied via the likelihood ratio that exists between an original and modified likelihood distribution. Here, the original, can be obtained by diverse analytical formulas, which are exact for the probability distribution. Hence through this method you can make sure that paths, which have their probabilities arbitrarily enhanced through changes of probability distribution, can be biased with a lower weight and hence this variant gets reduced.

Problems in pricing arithmetic average Asian options using Monte Carlo methods

There are a lot of researches, which depict the problem of pricing arithmetic average Asian options, via use of the Monte Carlo simulation techniques. Hence before applications of these techniques, there is a need to implement a background and be aware of its usage. With Monte Carlo simulation, the option values may be regarded as just estimators, and so there is a need for searching a judicious choice of control variates. These variates would help to enhance pricing presentation of simulation, which is critical. Getting closed form solutions with European option and geometric average Asian option, there is a need to use control variates.

Basically results on these equations have revealed that applying the geometric average Asian option, as a control variate for Monte Carlo approach, helps to improve the standard deviation result. This also helps in providing a narrower confidence interval. A check on the antithetic variate method had also been implemented, which revealed that the variance reduction technique had been less attractive as compared to the geometric Asian option variate. There are also various arguments revealing the fact that the arithmetic average Asian call option has lesser value less, than or equal to its corresponding European call.

A major disadvantage of the Monte Carlo methods would be its path dependent options and large number of calculations. These are both necessary for updating the path dependent variables via simulation. In this case, control variate methods also exhaust their capacity here and methods like the Quasi Monte Carlo methods are suggested. The Quasi-random or the low-discrepancy methods are based on the idea of not generating these sample paths arbitrarily, and let the focus be on systematically means, with complete deterministic notions. The select points available in the probability areas would be optimally filling up this space. So, assortment of points should be in a lesser discrepancy sequence, like the Sobol sequence. Also noting the average of a derivative payoff, with points in less discrepancy sequence, would prove to be more efficient, instead of getting the averages of any payoff at haphazard points.

Vorst approximation and its role in options

Basically Asian options use various methods for approximation of risks, instruments and portfolios. So there are vast categories of number of approximation methods available for dealing with the issues of price of average rate options. Here the considerations in evaluations include the underlying asset, which may be either in form of currency or equity. There are so many realistic pricing models that help to r average interest rate caps. These realistic pricing models are based on inter-bank offered rates, which are often not published.

Some of the proposed methods here include those of Levy in 1992, Vorst in 1992, also termed as Vorst approximation and the Rogers and Shi method of 1995. These are the suggested methods which may be adapted for getting average rate options and compare them with price average interest rate caps. A comparison of their computational efficiencies would benefit if getting these evaluations. There are basically different ways to implement these equations, but with concern with options, all of these three methods are very fast. The Vorst approximation method is often preferred over the Monte Carlo simulation. The other two methods used here are also quick enough for on-the-fly calculations.

An important factor here would to know more about the underlying interest rate model, which is used on a consistent basis and is observed with term structure of the interest rate. Thus one of the most suggested models here would be the Vorst approximations that had been developed for practical implementation.

But it has been seen that as far as the financial literature proceeds, the Vorst model does provide approximate solutions to deal with equations. The Vorst model had been proposed by its author in 1992 and has been named after him. The proposed model is actually an approximation of the value, based on mathematical mean rate option, which is calculated through analytical solution of a numerical mean rate option. But it has been seen that this value of the geometric mean would always be equal or less than the value of an arithmetic mean. Hence this method often introduces a bias or prejudice into the estimate.

Hence, it has been stated by many financial experts that the price given by the Vorst approximation may often lower the limit of any financial prospects to the value of the option. But methods have been devised to correct this bias and so the Vorst proposes modifying the strike price to get rid of this prejudice. Financial experts have observed that the transaction costs rise with flow, but it has been seen that this increase is more than often not an appreciable one. The increase with drift occurs from one point to another and hence becomes the appreciable intended for a change. It can be assumed here that the transaction costs would mainly depend on changes in the delta value, which can be estimated by Vorst approximations. Hence these would also provide for the changes in the value of the underlying security.

But on the other context it has been noticed that as the drift parameter grows, there is a higher value of the underlying security, on an average. This further implies an increase or rise in the value of each adjustment. But on the other hand it also means that as the drift grows in absolute value, there would be dispersion of the value, for underlying security, which increases too. Thus this increase in dispersion states that the related movements in the delta value, amid each adjustment would be bigger when the drift is increasingly negative. This implies in negative connotations for the negative drifts and increasingly positive connotations for the positive drift.

Many of the financial experts had been spending time researching and studying the involvement of the element, which had contributed to a slight reduction of transaction costs. This happens as volatility increases, but is not present there and thus the given constant volatility can be used for the Vorst evaluation. Basically a rise or growth in the dispersion of delta values would be in accordance with the reflected growth in transaction costs. According to the 1990 Vorst model, there had been a demonstration of the geometric average option, which would be highly correlated with the arithmetic average option.

There is a lot of importance given to sampling and stratification here, along with the models provided by Glasserman, Heidelberger and Shahabuddin in 1990, which have been considered for an application to Asian options. These models, along with Vorst approximation has been known for significantly reducing the variance. Financial experts have used the knowledge of the Vorst model for deriving a lower bound for the value of an Asian option. Here the model and its author have used the knowledge about the geometric average always being smaller than or equal to its equivalent average.

The Vorst model had been desirable to check the value of arithmetic Eurasian fixed strike call that is bounded below due to its geometric counterpart. In this reference many other models like that of Curran in 1992 and 1994, and Rogers and Shi in 1995, had successfully managed in getting a very tight lower bound by conditioning and applying inequality theories. The result was getting lower bound with a better estimate of the option value as compared to a huge number of analytical approximations.

There are two approximations that can help to size the error with financial estimates and these include that of Vorst and the recently added Vyncke, Goovaerts and Dhaene in 2004. Basically the Vorst approximation helps in the essential approximation of the arithmetic average as a constant, with the geometric average as plus. Here the constant would be determined if the first moment coincides with the arithmetic average.

Asian options and market research

Asian Options are defined as the options whose payouts are dependent on the average price of the underlying asset. This is done over a specific period and it is mainly for the life of the option. Any Asian option can be broadly categorized into two main categories, which are the average price options that payoff at maturity and are equal to the average price of its underlying asset, within a limited period, subtracting its fixed strike price for the option. On the other hand the average strike option has a payoff, which is equal to the price of its underlying asset at expiry, but reduces its variable strike. This price is i equal to the average price for their underlying assets over a period.

Like the European options, even the Asian options have been structured to be exercised at maturity but there are some unique structures of this option that allow them to be exercised anytime. The payouts here are based on average to-date costs of their underlying assets. Calculations of the Asian option are simple and they are numerically characterizing the costs for any kind of arithmetically averaged Asian option. Basically the Asian approach mutually includes continuously and discretely sampled options. These may be extended to get the incessant or discrete dividend yields.

As compared to most of the current day methods, the Asian option does not require implementing or jumping conditions for sampling or dividend days. These Asian options are securities that would pay off depending on the average of the underlying stock price after a certain period. There is actually no general analytical solution for the price of the Asian option and there are basically a variety of techniques developed to analyze arithmetic average for Asian options.

There are many financial experts who had devised approximations to get closed form expressions, which include recent papers by Thompson in 1999. Here the Asian option has been provided with tight analytical bounds to get the option price. Some other researches had been conducted by Geman and Yor in 1993 and computed transformation of prices for continuously sampled Asian option. The numerical inversion continues to remain a problematic issue for low volatility or for the short maturity cases.

Recently Linetsky had derived a new integral formula for the costs of continuously sampled Asian option in 2000. This has again become a slow convergent for low volatility cases. In most of the Asian option calculations the Monte Carlo simulation works well and this cannot be computationally costly without the enhancement of variance lessening techniques. In these researches there is a basic requirement for getting account for the inherent discrimination bias, which results from the approximation of continuous time processes, done via discrete sampling by experts like Broadie, Glasserman and Kou, in the year 1999.

Hence it may be stated that the prices for an Asian option could be found by solving a partial differential equation or the PDE, with two space dimensions. This would be prone to oscillatory solutions along with observations of two-dimensional PDE for a floating strike Asian option, which can be reduced to a one-dimensional PDE. Other experts like Rogers and Shi in 1995 had formulated a one-dimensional PDE. This Asian option could be floating and fixed strike, where the one dimensional

PDE is more difficult to solve numerically. This happens because of the diffusion on term is very minute for values of interest on the finite difference grid. An attempt to improve the numerical performance of the same has been done by Andreasen.

Many efforts have been made to try unifying pricing techniques for different types of options and then relating these methods to pricing Asian option. These include methods by Lipton in 1999, which had witnessed similarity of pricing equations for the passport and Asian option. Some other techniques had been developed for pricing options on a traded account. This could be done by including all options that replicated through a self-financing trading in the underlying asset.

There are various techniques for pricing contracts available too, with many experts developing alternative frameworks for pricing a variety of options using methods like scale invariance. Then there are also the more general semi-analytic solutions available for prices of continuously sampled Asian options.

Simple and unifying approach for pricing Asian options can be discrete and continuous arithmetic average. Here the one dimensional PDE be easily implemented to give tremendously fast and accurate results for pricing of these options. The approach also uses instances of continuous or discrete dividends.

When compared to other methods, the popular techniques for pricing Asian options mainly constitute the Monte Carlo simulation, along with the numerical inversion of the Laplace transform and the alternative PDE methods of Rogers and Shi. These are techniques that can also be improved with time and changes may be seen in these methods in the coming years.

Restrictions of certain models in Asian options

Even though the Monte Carlo simulation can provide for accurate results for all choices of parameters, many financial experts believe that the speed of Monte Carlo simulation can be enhanced by certain choice of control variates. This method is still considered inherently and computationally unviable for pricing Asian options.

Since all present techniques are either computationally unstable, they may often get very slow or complicated to implement. Thus it has been seen that there is actually no single technique that has been widely accepted to price Asian options in concern with all choices of market parameters.

But in contrast, some of the methods presented in recent times have proved to be satisfactory and a stable choice for all parameters. These also include the small volatilities and short maturities to give accurate results within 6 decimal digits. This can be done in less than a second of computation time and hence the newer methods are now being implemented in Asian options for determining risks and pricing. There are various numerical results of techniques by the Monte-Carlo methods which show that the PDE method suggested was consistent in getting these numbers. The benefit of the method presented is that it can also be used to price discretely sampled Asian option.

Some of the benefits of new calculations and formulas include continuously sampled Asian options with consistent results, within a second of computation time.

The other benefit here would be flexibility of these methods that can be considered as discretely sampled Asian call option. These methods help to derive factors like dividend payment that result in lower Asian option price. Compared to newer methods, the Monte Carlo technique took more than 10 minutes to get the stimulation implementation with control variate reduction.

The pricing of the American style option cannot be done through this method because there is a need to track both the stock price and its running average, which again requires the two-dimensional formulation of the problem. Thus the case of the American Asian option may not be reduced to one dimension because of the fixed strike involved.

Asian options with Forex brokers

The Forex option brokers are mainly categorized mainly into two unique categories which include Forex brokers. These brokers offer online option platforms for trading and the brokers who provide trading option via telephone, where trades are placed through brokerage desk. Usually trading account minimal requirements vary from some thousand dollars, and go up to more than fifty thousand dollars, depending on your options. There are certain Asian option brokers who need investors for trading certain Forex options contracts with least notional values or their contract sizes of a margin of almost $500,000. Also the Forex option contracts tend to get entered, or even exit at any given time, while some sorts of Forex option contracts restrict your cash till termination or settlement.

Hence, the kind of Forex option contract selected by you would be a determining factor here. Before trading or investing in Asian options you should try to inquire with the Forex option brokers on factors like the preliminary trading financial credit minimums, contract liquidity and minimum duration of the contract. There is a need for all investors to comprehend definitely dissimilar risk characteristics that are involved in Asian option trading yield.

Usually the plain vanilla options refer to normal put and call contracts of options, which are traded via the exchange. But when you are dealing with the Forex option trading, this would imply general option contracts. These are usually traded over the counter ones, or even those done by OTC through some Forex dealer, and at times a clearinghouse. Hence, this deal can be termed as purchasing, or selling, of a typical Forex call option or put option contracts. Very restricted brokers provide for plain vanilla Forex options available online with a real time quote of twenty four hours a day. Usually the option brokers are dealing via telephone and here the vanilla Forex options provide good liquidity for Asian options.

The vanilla Forex option contracts are available for combination used with each other or with some mark Forex contracts, where they form basic or multifaceted Forex trading strategies.

There are exotic Forex options broker too but it should be kept in mind that there are dissimilar Forex definitions of exotic. In the first connotation the description of a Forex exotic can be referring to any distinct currency, which can be less traded than many of the other major currencies. Some other connotation would be referring to the website of Forex option agreement or the trading strategy, which is actually a derivative of typical vanilla option contract.

There is a need to understand exotic Forex options along with non-vanilla options. The regular vanilla Forex options generally have certain expiration structures along with payout arrangement and amounts. But the exotic Forex option contracts have some or all changes, as compared to the vanilla Forex option. These exotic options are mainly used in the Asian options market and they are tailored to meet the specific investor needs via a broker, with least chances of liquidity.

The exotic Forex options may be traded by profitable and institutional depositors instead of the regular Forex traders. The exotic Forex options mostly include Asian options or even the average price options, along with barrier options. In the barrier options your payout would depend on the fact whether the underlying would reach a convinced price level. In this reference the exotic Forex options or Asian options would also include baskets where the payout would depend on multiple currencies along with binary options where payout is cash, or even nothing, in case the underlying cannot reach the strike price.

There are various look back options to be considered here which include the factors where the payout has been based on the highest or least amount prices, which are attained in the course of life or duration of the contract. Compound options can be referred to the options that have numerous strikes and implementation dates. Apart from these one can also find chooser options, spread options, packages etc. which have a vital role in these exotic options.

It should be remembered that since these exotic options are tailored their contract types modify and evolve with time to meet requirements of these always changing needs. The exotic Forex options contracts tend to focus on tailored requirements of the individual investor. Hence most Asian options businesses have transaction through the telephone or even via Forex option brokers.

It has been seen that there are some Forex option brokers that provide for single Forex options contracts via online modes. Here an investor can spell out the required amount that he or she wants to risk in exchange for a specified payout. This would again depend on how far the underlying cost reaches or its expected strike price.

These transactions are obtainable by legitimate Forex brokers, who work online, and can be regarded as a kind of Asian option. However, premiums priced for certain kinds of contracts may also result in higher plain vanilla option contracts. These contracts would have comparable strike prices and the investors are not able to sell out of their option place, if they have invested in such options.

The only way to get rid of this offset position would be through different kinds of risk management means or strategies. This can also be done as trade-off to get or select the specified amount, which an investor wants to risk, according to the payout they want to achieve. Hence the basic idea of this would be to reimburse a premium and give up liquidity. Thus investors considering Asian options should compare available premiums before you invest, and ensure that their brokerage firms are reputable.

For investors it is fairly effortless for entering an Asian option contract, but they should be confident about the kind of contract they are opting for. Many exotic Forex options provide for betting, which may not be legitimate. There are many Asian option firms that have off-shore bodies or they may also be located in other remote locations. Many of these are not actually Forex brokerage offices or firms and don't fall under regulation any government organization. Hence those who are considering investments in concern with the Asian options should choose brokerage firms that are legitimate.

But whenever investments are made in an Asian option or mutual fund or bond, the investors are charged a commission. In the Forex market, options do not involve payment of commission and here investors are able to pay what they see. Basically the broker would be earning the difference between the buy and ask spread. In the Forex market an investor can be allowed to trade in very high leverage, which can also go up to 1:400. Hence the investor can control about $100,000 with investments of amounts like $250.

Investors can make their money work harder with Asian options in the Forex market. But even though there is the leverage of high gains, the Asian options in Forex markets would also lead to higher losses.

With the increased leverage a lot of people say that investing in Forex market would be very risky. Though the amount of leverage may seem aggressive, the Forex market provides an apt antidote of risks and profits. With Asian options in Forex market, the investors have the potential to determine the price with which they want to enter a trade. They are also able to determine the price at which they would like to make their exit.

There are provisions for certain guaranteed stops in the market, and these allow you to specify the exact amount that you are willing to risk, and what is not possible in the stock market. The Forex market for Asian options gives you an opportunity to deal with better investments.

Asian market options and the role of insurance

It can be said that options are traded in their own right, and they may also be traded as insurance for an additional trade like that of a stock trade. There are options that can be traded as insurance, which is also known as hedging. Here the option protects its underlying deal by limiting a certain quantity of potential loss. Trading options in reference with insurance may prove to be very useful. However, there are many traders that fail to appreciate how options indemnity works, and thus they hesitate to use it.

Basically the options can be traded as insurance for various sectors and this also includes the Asian option market. Investors can know more about this trading by getting the fundamentals of trading options as insurance. This would enable them to understand if which options trades can be used for the related underlying trades.

The insurance options works in many different ways where the options trade make insurance, like another trade. These are always long option trades where the purchasing is either a call or a put. Hence the options trade also ensures limited risk, where the utmost loss is the price of the option, also known as the premium. Basically the maximum loss of an option trade would become the maximum loss for its underlying trade. This replaces the potentially unlimited and much larger loss of its underlying trade.

For instance, if a long trade for some individual stock had been completed by buying a thousand shares for $30, then the potential loss for the concerned trade would be set at 1000 shares x $30, per share = $30,000. With the options insurance trade and investor can buy ten put options, where each of these options would be worth about 100 shares. The strike price would be about $30 and so these ten put options would cost $1,000 for 10 options, at the cost of $100 per option. So the loss here would only of $1,000 for the combined stockpile and options trade rather than the potential $30,000 loss for a given stock.

Basically the reasons for the dramatic reduction in risk would be the fact that put option permits a holder to sell off their stocks at the strike price. If you are buying a stock a particular price and selling it at the same price, then there would be no profit. So with these trade options as insurance the loss would only be the cost of the insurance, which would imply higher savings for you.

The options insurance trades consist of long options trades or the buying options, along with the money options. For getting a long stock trade insures there would be a need to use long put options trade. For insuring a short stock trade, there would be the need of a long call options trade would be used. It can be said that in the long stock trade the options trade would be long, with put type and a strike price, which would be the same as the stock purchase price.

The short stock trade would be including long trade options with call type and the strike price here would be the same as the stock purchase cost.

It has been seen that many European and Asian traders would also build options insurance trades via the use of warrants or warrant insurance trades. Since these warrants have reduced premiums, when compared to options, they are preferred way to for making insurance trades for non US traders, especially Asians.

There is a need to make sure that insurance trades using warrants are identical to making insurance trades, with the use of options. However, there are diversities amid options and warrants, which should be considered and taken into account for better evaluation. For instance, a common dissimilarity between options and warrants would be the fact that warrant multipliers are potentially used in a different way from options multipliers.

Asian options and the global financial market

The arithmetic Asian or average price option provides for payoffs based on the average underlying price, which is mostly specified for a time period. These Asian options are vital for the family of derivative contracts and offer a wide variety of applications. These applications are then used in forms of currency, interest rate, commodity, equity, energy, and insurance markets.

There are basically two analytical formulas available to get the value of the continuously sampled mathematical Asian option, in concern with their underlying asset price. This can be done using the geometric Brownian motion where experts are able to identity in law amid the essential of geometric Brownian motion, but for a period of finite time. This equation would state the time of a one-dimensional diffusion process through affine drift and linear diffusion. Thus it would express Asian option values considering its spectral expansions, which have often been associated with the diffusion infinitesimal generator.

The main formula here would be the infinite series of terms that involve Whittaker functions M and W. Another formula would be the single real integral of an expression that involves Whittaker function W plus, in regards with some parameter values, and the finite number of extra terms involving unfinished gamma functions and the Laguerre polynomials. So these two formulas are allowing an accurate computation of incessantly sampled arithmetic Asian option prices.

The Asian average price options offer investors with payoffs that are based on the average underlying price. This can also be termed as their financial variable over a prior specified time period. In the Asian-style derivatives, there is a vital role of the wide variety of applications that had been first introduced by Boyle and Emanuel in the year 1980.

Basically there is an array of economic and financial reasons for these Asian options to get so popular. When developing long term economic projections and corporate treasurers would be worried about the average foreign exchange rate, or the commodity price, they realized the importance of its accounting period. Hence it can be stated that an average rate or average price option would be a natural corporate financial tool, which would help in risk management. Apart from this factor, the module provided for a typically less expensive option, as compared to the standard options in concern with volatility over the average exchange rate. This applied to the instances where the commodity price would be less than the volatility rate or the price itself.

For getting the specific example of the same, many multinational corporations use the average rate foreign exchange options as a basis tool for hedging their net revenue exposures. Through the processes like hedging, a company policy can hedge its entire budgeted revenue in a given quarter. In concern with foreign exchange exposures one can get an average rate option to maintain stable earnings quarter after quarter.

The second application here would be exploiting the fact that it is possible for a large market participant to influence the cost of a thinly traded commodity, and that on any particular day. Hence it can be stated that it would be very difficult to manipulate an average price over a period of time. Hence a lot of international companies prefer the contracts, which are Asian-style. These contracts have a settled based on the average price of a commodity, for a particular duration. This also involves the period preceding contract expiration.

Many of the corporate mergers and takeovers also prefer the average price contingent and use the accurate and precise pricing of Asian options. This is vital to deal with the practical of financial engineering. The issue of financial engineering with other modules had also lead to many interesting methodological issues. Since these options are path-dependent, prices of an Asian option, for any given time, would be the function of both the prices, including underlying assets at that time and average of the rising underlying prices till that period.

The other factor to adhere to is that Asian style option, or the average style option, is actually a form of security with a payoff. This would be largely dependant on the average of a quantity of index price level, and range over a period of time. It is said that the first OTC trades in Asian options took place in the 1980s. But today the Asian style options have emerged as an exotic form of European style option, and that too with the possibilities of a single exercise date. These Asian options are now the most commonly traded form of Exotic Option.

Understanding the Forex Trader's Psychology

Forex trading begins in the mind. The investor who trades in currency should have the correct mindset. Ed Ponsi who is a renowned professional trader emphasizes in his books and conferences about the correct trading mindset. In his famous summit at Furama City he said that Forex trading is a combination of 55 percent state of mind, 30 percent money management and 15 percent of strategy and voila you have the correct combination for Forex trading

This Furama City centre was established in 2006 and is pioneers in Forex education in Singapore and Asia. The pioneers of this institute wanted to create awareness about Forex trading and the potentials about the Forex. Hence the institute offers a training course on Forex trading for new and experienced traders. Mr. Ponsi is often called by the institute to lecture on Forex trading strategies. His seminars are a great among the students.

Mr. Ponsi is known for charming his audience with his wit and wisdom. He believes that a Forex trader always starts with a plan, these plans act as a travel map like in case of a traveler. He advised his seminar participants that Forex traders should start and stop before entering a trade. Once you start making plans and introspection you can minimize your losses and also ease your stress.

Well surely none of us like losses, and its best to plan your actions. But we often see that the traders make wrong decision and are egoistic to accept their wrong decision. It is important and better to accept your wrong decision and make amends immediately instead of holding on to it for very long. By holding on to the wrong trade you will increase your loses. If you are quick you can make gains and be in a winning situation. Especially the bullish traders who feel that the market would rise should be adaptable to any situation and should be very prompt while trading.

Traders who blame others or look for excuses for defending their losses never succeed. The traders need to take the responsibility of their actions to be successful in their business. Once you are analytical in your trade you will be successful and also be able to achieve your goals. Forex traders should not trade impulsively or through their emotions but with their plan and analytical ideas. Also over confidence can ruin your trade, so it's best to trade with an open mind and make the correct decision.

Put your ego in the last when trading in Forex

The Forex market trades three trillion U.S dollars every day and there is no space for your personal ego. If you give your ego a lot of importance and don't make rapid changes then you might face severe losses as the market is very volatile. Many traders get swayed by emotion but what is important in Forex trading is consistency and discipline. One needs to follow structured trading plan and trade with proper risk management to minimize your risk and losses. The trader needs to understand that money management and trading psychology is the key to success.

- Understanding Losses

If you are experiencing losses, then probably it's time for you to review your trading plan. A series of losses can easily de motivate anyone, and hence it's best to follow rules and not get influenced by emotion when trading in Forex as a lot of money goes into it.

- Ego

This often seen among trader and especially among ace traders who don't make the changes as they feel that their decision is correct, even when it's a wrong financial move. The egoistic traders are so desperate to prove their point that they don't make the required changes and the Forex market makes you pay for it. The ego is big hindrance that prevents you from making big. You need to change to improve, instead you try to defend your action which can lead to heavy losses. You should not pit your ego in a Forex trading market as huge amount of money is involved and readily make changes wherever necessary.

- Inconsistency

Do not trade according to your whim and fancy. An inconsistent trade can kill your motivation and also your trade. When you trade with an inconsistent pattern, you count on your luck more strongly and you might have to pay for your inconsistent trading behavior.

What is support and resistance?

Support and resistance are the two major tools in day trading analysis method used by all the traders. It is important to understand both the concepts very well. Support can be regarded as the floor for the price. The buying pressure in this area exceeds the selling pressure and automatically the prices are pushed upwards.

When trading in the Forex market, are you trading with support of resistance is the most obvious question. To be able to trade in the Forex market, and to increase your trading success you surely need a string support system. The support in this context is the community of likeminded traders, a structured system to coach new traders as well as matured traders.

If the support is right the trader can easily pick up the nuances of the trade and can start saving time as well as start making profit. This support system also acts as a backbone for the intermediate trader; they are able to correct themselves especially when a bad habit creeps in.

The mature trader utilizes the support system and treats it as medium to share his trading experiences with the new trader.

When building a support system you need to keep in mind three important factors:
- Mentor
- Attitude
- Platform

The mentor is the coach or the guide to help new traders in the Forex trading. He /she world help the new traders take better decision by giving valuable advice based on his/her experience. You can decide whether a trader is capable of being a mentor by reviewing his / her personal records or trading credentials.

Attitude is the next most important thing in this dynamic trade, you need to make most of the learning experience and above all be ready to make change and open to learning. You need to be flexible, and also remember that attitude determines altitude. When you have great attitude you can grow to a great extent.

Platform is the stand where new traders can discuss their problems and also learn about new trading rules. It regulates whether the new traders are able to attend classes or not. With the help of online support system traders are able access information and trading tips within a few clicks. The platform acts as a one stop solution arena for all new and matured traders for any enquiry regarding Forex trading.

To start a career in Forex trading

 Last year (2009) during the recession phase, the world monitory reserves and central banks had started taking emergency measures. The credit had tightened and the job market worsened and who can forget the layoffs. People had started looking at alternative means of income and hence Forex came to their rescue. But not many understand what Forex trading is; they probably have heard it a million time but don't really know the meaning. Forex trading as the name suggests is the buying and selling of foreign currency, but there is more to it than this simple definition. These currencies can be traded through a broker or a dealer and are executed in pairs. For instance the Singapore dollar can be paired with Malaysian Ringgit, and similarly US dollar and Japanese Yen can categorised simultaneously. The Forex market is huge and is growing at a very fast pace, the trading value of Forex is more than four trillion US dollars.

One can make profit from Forex trading by cashing onto the difference in the exchange rates. But this market is really volatile and you need to act very quickly. FX trading depends on the movement of the FX rates. The trade can be one for very short term and sometimes for very long duration.

The fluctuations in the Forex prices are determined by various factors. Some of the factors are international economic scenario, international political situations, and level of interest rate. The traders in the Forex market include, central and commercial banks, hedge funds, large business house and individual traders.

Advantages of Forex trading

It is a 24 hour market, and is accessible to trader from any part of the world .The main gadgets required in Forex trading is mobile phone and laptop with a internet connection and you can trade from any part of the world. There are no restrictions on trading, if a trader believes that the currency would depreciate then he is free to sell, but if it's held for more than a day then you need to consider the carrying cost. This surely indicates that potential profit exists. The Forex trading market has an equal trading field for all and information is available on the net unlike equity trading where the traders and analysts have an upper hand in the trade.

Forex Education

For new traders or for people who want to plunge into Forex trading can get to know the basic of the trade from the FXI academy.

The Foreign Exchange Academy offers a much formatted course for individual traders, and also teaches techniques and tools in this front so that they can become professional traders. The FXI Academy in Singapore also has offices in Penang, Jaya and Petaling. They academy teaches prudent money management tools, strategies to its students. It advocates three main aspects of trading money management, strategy and correct state of mind. The trader should apply prudent money management tools when trading as this helps in saving and managing your capital and long term investment goals.

The strategy is the way and is the key to profit from the market. These strategies are based on examining market trend, market range, reversal, breakout, arbitrage and hedging. These strategies are unique to the academy and can be used in a combination of trader's personality and state of mind. One should trade with an open and positive mind as negative attitude will surely cause trouble.

Conclusion

Planning to trade your money in the Forex Trade? For this, it is important to understand the different concepts and terms used in the Forex market. Here's a little guide:

The Forex market trades USD3.5 trillion in a single day from all over the world. It has become the largest financial market of the world. Money, of course is the most basic necessity for all and you want to be sure about where it is going. You should know how the Forex Trade is executed and how money is made or lost.

The first concept to understand here is to know how to read a pair of currencies since Forex currencies are always displayed in pairs. For example: USD/JPY or USD/INR or AUD/CHF.
The currency on the left is the "base currency" and the currency on the right is the "counter currency" in a currency pair. The base currency is always taken as one and is expressed as a value of the counter currency. Like:

- USD/INR = 44.273 (1 Dollar is equivalent to 44.273 Rupees)
- USD/CAD = 1.5055 (1 Dollar is equivalent to 1.5055 Canadian dollars)

So when you see a quote showing EUR/USD = 1.4150, you will quickly understand three things:

1. EUR is the base currency
2. USD is the counter currency
3. 1 EURO is equal to 1.4150 US Dollars

Long and Short

If the trader feels that prices are going to rise, he would execute a "Long" and this would be a 'buy' trade.

Similarly if the trader feels that prices are going to fall, he would execute a "Short" and this would then become a 'sell' trade.

How does a trader execute a trade?

For example:

If a trader executes a 'Long' trade at say 41.50 because he feels that the price will rise, 41.50 will be his entry price.

He now decides to exit the trade at a rate of 43.50. This will become his Profit Target.

Now, in another case, if the trader executes a 'Short' trade at 42.60 because he feels that the price will fall, 42.60 will be his entry price.

He decides to exit the trade at 40.20. This is his Profit Target.

This example clearly shows that in 'Long' trade, the profit target is more than the entry price (43.50>41.50). On the other hand, in a 'Short' trade, the profit target is less than the entry price (40.20<42.60).

Another term that is commonly used in the Forex trade is a pip. A 'pip' usually refers to the smallest movement on the chart. The little change in the rate of a currency is termed as pip. For example, if the quote of USD/INR moves from 44.273 to 44.275, we say the movement is 2 pips. The difference between the original price and the changed price is calculated in terms of pips.

It is important to note here that whenever the Japanese Yen appears as the counter currency, the second decimal becomes the pip. This is because the price of Japanese currency is quoted to 2 decimal places and other currencies are quoted till 4 decimal places. So for other currencies, the fourth decimal is the pip.

www.ingramcontent.com/pod-product-compliance
Lightning Source LLC
Chambersburg PA
CBHW070228210526
45169CB00023B/1441